GIRLS IT'S TIME FOR A CHANGE

The Girls Guide To Puberty

Author : **Joan Reid**
Design and Layout : **WorldTech**
Cover page and Illustrations : **Carolina Storni**

Published by
10-10-10 Publishing
122-445 Apple Creek Blvd.
Markham, Canada
L3R 9X7

London, England, United Kingdom
www.girlsitstimeforachnage.com

ISBN: 978-1634437950

E: joanre29@gmail.com | M: +44 (0)7947158537

For information about special discounts for bulk purchases, please contact 10-10-10 Publishing at 1-888-504-6257

Printed in the United States of America

Dedicated to my daughter Taymah, with love.
If it wasn't for you there would be no book.

ABOUT THE AUTHOR

Joan Reid lives in London, England. She is both a microbiologist and a sexual health promotional speaker. This makes her uniquely qualified to discuss all things relating to science and the body. The book was originally given to her daughter Taymah, as a gift to help her make an easier transition from that of a child to becoming a confident young woman. Joan had found it difficult to locate a book that gave a no holds barred approach regarding what a girl would experience when she entered puberty. She wanted to answer those questions that so many girls ask, but for the most part have to fumble alone without really understanding how their body's work. Why are these changes necessary for a girl's development? Is a typical question that Joan herself asked? In addition she wanted to give her daughter tips and advice to overcome the obstacles that she would undoubtedly face as she grew up.

After reading *Girls It's Time for A Change, The Girls Guide to Puberty,* her daughter challenged her to publish it, and so "Girls it's Time for a Change" came into being. Joan wishes that girls around the world will use her book, to prepare themselves for all that puberty and their period will bring. Understanding that the change in mind and body are a necessary part of growing up, and hopes that "Girls it's Time for a Change" will help the reader fully appreciate and love what being a woman is all about.

ACKNOWLEDGEMENTS

TO MY MOTHER, MRS LUCILLE Reid, thank you for your patience, your love and your willingness to look after your granddaughter.

To my brothers, T Reid and Lloyd Reid, my sisters, Vanessa Reid, Beulett Hunter, Rhoena Mitchell and Stephanie Nicolson. My family, my love.

To my other sisters and brothers, Rosemarie Samuels (Precious), Judy Samuels, Pamela Williams, Carol Mathieu, Debra Ambrose, Sherrall Burrows, Joann Graham-Delisser, Hermine Graham, Grace Chambers, my prayer Partner Ruth Chambers, Myrtle O'Keefe, Glenda Grant , Jennifer Constantine, Lorna Mckenzie, Jeninfer St Louis-McKenzie, Janet Pilgrim, Stephen McKenzie, Kenneth Mckenzie, Winston McKenzie Richard Delisser, David Mathieu and Curtis Bruce, what would I do without you all in my life? I thank

God for the times we spent together growing up. Such a blessing that our lives are interwoven, never to be separated.

To my school friends, Patricia White, Healther Collymore, Joyce Hickson, Annette Curtis, Sonia McKenzie, Pamela Smith, Wendy John Baptiste, Laura Richmond, and the one and only Rosemarie King. Haggerston. Girls, we had fun despite everything.

To my other mothers, Mrs Samuels, Miss Ann Williams, Miss Cheryl Brown, Mrs Merchant , Mrs Annis Mahbeer, Mrs Doreen Williams, Ms Yvonne Waithe, Mrs Constantine and Mrs Edwards as well as the congregation of the Stokenewington and Hackney SDA Churches.

I mention those in my life who are gone but will never be forgotten.

My hero and father Mr. Valentine Reid, I miss you Daddy, every day. Miss Patricia Campbell, tears still flow; Miss Sonia Murray, after so many years it still hurts to lose you. Sis Lawrence, I still miss that quick wit and your laugh. Annette Graham and her mother Mrs Carmen Graham, and my Aunty Mrs Ruth Acey, a powerhouse of love and encouragement who died this March 2016. You are greatly missed.

It takes a village to raise a child.

There are those you meet along your life's journey who influence your thinking and mindset and challenge you in a way that makes you feel uncomfortable with being you in your current state. They instill the knowledge that there is so much more to you than who you are now, and at the same time give you the tools you need to fulfill your purpose. I would like to acknowledge the following people who have done just that for me.

To Miss Carolina Storni my beautiful, talented artist and illustrator. Thank you for all your hard work your beautiful pictures enabled my words to come alive as your strove to capture all that I wanted to say.

To Naval Kumar, author, digital marketer, entrepreneur, my mentor and book architect, co-owner of Brand Marketer and so much more in the future, thank you for your help, and your gentle but persistent prodding and encouragement. I am really blessed to have met you.

Chinmai Swamy, author, product developer, international transformational coach, unintentional funny guy and co-owner of Brand Marketer, thank you so much. Isn't it amazing that you can know someone for a short time who already has been such an influence? Thank you for your advice. I know I will be working with you again and again.

Paul Lynch, CEO of My Dot Com Business, thank you for being such a warm and welcoming person who is willing to share and even drop me an email now and again, even though you are busy running such a successful group of companies.

Alex Jefferies, CEO of Working With Alex, wow, your energy and drive to motivate and empower is amazing. You have been a great influence on me since you have mentored me. Your Working with Alex course is fantastic.

Matt Lloyd, CEO of MOBE, it was great meeting with you in Thailand last year; I had a fantastic time. It has been wonderful doing business with you; I have learnt so much.

John Lee, CEO of Wealth Dragons and author of "Wealth Dragons Way," thank you so much for your help and advice.

To Raymond Aaron, CEO of 10-10-10 program and author of Chicken Soup for the Parent's Soul and Chicken Soup for the Canadian Soul. From the first time you walked onto that stage in Thailand I knew I'd be working with you; you are a giant in a small frame. Your wit and humor had me in stitches, but with the humor came knowledge. Your encouragement has enabled me to get to this stage. All I can say is that your gift has changed thousands of lives, including mine, and I thank you. May God continue to bless you and your family as you continue to enrich people's lives with your special gift of learning through humor and keeping it REAL.

FOREWORD

JOAN REID'S BOOK, GIRLS IT'S Time for A Change, is one my wife and I wish we had had when our girls were growing up. I found myself nodding and saying, " That's so true," "Oh that's the reason" or "I wish I had been aware of that; I would have handled this or that situation so much better." Girls It's Time for A Change is a delightful, easy to read and understand book that helps your daughter make that transition from girl to young woman, as it removes the uncertainty of growing up by giving clarity to a subject that a lot of parents find difficult to talk about.

The book is full of information that every girl needs. It answers questions every girl might want to ask, but feels embarrassed to voice. What I like about the book is that it encourages your daughters to seek advice from their mothers and even us fathers. Her chapter "It's Good to Talk" gently explains why it is important to seek advice, and it prepares you to be their go to expert.

Joan's background, not just as a mother but also as a scientist, has enabled her to peel away the scientific jargon and present the biology surrounding puberty in a way that is so simple to understand.

Joan's chapter titles such as "Cry Me a River," "Beauty and the Beast" and 'It's a Sweaty Affair" will resonate with the parent and intrigue the young lady. Her goal is to put girls who read the book at ease as they grow up, giving tips and advice that they will undoubtedly need as they navigate their way through puberty and adolescence.

I highly recommend that you read Girls It's Time For A Change, the girls guide to puberty, as you will learn a lot and help your daughter as she grows into the wonderful person she is destined to be.

—Raymond Aaron
New York Times Top 10 Best Selling Author

TABLE OF CONTENTS

THE ANTICIPATION

I STARTED MY PERIOD WHEN I was thirteen and a half years old. It made its appearance while I was at school. I felt this strange urge to visit the bathroom even though I didn't need to pee.

I'd been looking forward to its arrival since I was eight years old. My friend Anna and I were the same age, but she had started just after her eighth birthday. Mrs. Creighton, the school nurse, would make a fuss over the girls who began their periods and had a supply of sanitary towels available in case we either started our periods or had run out.

Not one to be left out, but feeling as such, I would regularly proclaim that I had started my period, only to be turned away when asked to show her my underwear.

On my last attempt, I went into the art room and dabbed some red poster paint on my knickers to show her the proof. I recall to my embarrassment Mrs. Creighton trying but failing miserably to hold back the laughter that erupted when I showed her my knickers dripping with bright-red paint.

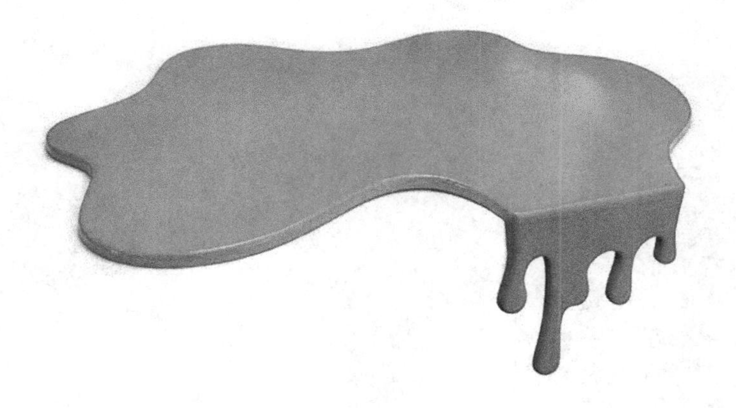

I can laugh now, but I was not laughing that day. Because of my antics, I had to go home knicker-less. Upon relaying the terrible events that had transpired that day to my mother, she started coughing in an attempt to conceal the laughter that kept surfacing. Both my Mum and Mrs. Creighton advised me not to rush to enter womanhood because it will be a life-changing experience. They both encouraged me to enjoy life and not to be in such a hurry to become older. I, however, thought it just wasn't fair, and longed to be like so many of my friends.

When my thirteenth birthday arrived, and nothing had happened, I secretly began to think something was wrong with me. It seemed everyone had started except me. It was almost a daily query from my girlfriends, who kept asking “the” question and making me feel as if I were abnormal. It seemed really exciting to be changing, and I felt left out.

So when the day eventually arrived I was ecstatic. I had joined the ranks of millions of girls around the world; I was normal, and I was becoming a woman. I liked the way my breasts were developing, and I looked forward to the other changes that I saw in my friends.

THE REALITY

The funny thing is, at the time I hadn't thought about why my friends who had started seeing their "monthlies" kept on asking me if "I had come on;" that was the phrase we used in those days. It wasn't until I started seeing my period that I understood the reasons for their constant questioning. It was because they were jealous, wishing they could turn back the clock, which is exactly how I felt.

Fast forward a few months after my dream had come true, and it became a nightmare; I hated it. The nausea, the pain, the stomach cramps and the bloating. The wearing of what I called miniature nappies, there were no ultra thin winged, adhesive strip sanitary pads in those days. They were sometimes over half an inch thick with a loop at either end, giving you the option to use a string belt to place through the loops and tie it around your waist, which would help keep the pad in place. I found this to be totally gross!

To top it off, the pad had a tendency to move out of place. There were a few occasions when a girl's pad would slip through her underwear, especially when playing games, which was so embarrassing. Although that never happened to me, I resorted to pinning the pad onto my knickers. I felt self-conscious because the pad's shape was clearly imprinted through my underwear, and I had to be careful what I wore. It was so uncomfortable at times, I rued the day I thought starting my period would be cool. I must have been nuts wanting to start my period at the age of eight. I felt like such an idiot for wanting to endure this kind of nuisance. I complained to my Mum and told her, in no uncertain terms, "I wanted my life back." She smiled;

I sensed she was in her mind's eye reliving the countless times I had complained about the unfairness of not being like my other friends. She hugged me and gave me some advice on how to cope; she told me how she felt when she started out, and reassured me, it would be fine.

CONGRATULATIONS AND COMMISERATIONS

SO FOR THOSE OF YOU who have started your period, congratulations and commiserations. I say that because your life is going to be just like that; a mixed bag. You'll experience the excitement, frustration, disappointments and anticipation. It's the exhilarating journey of life. You'll go through all these emotions and more, all rolled into one. You've got your whole life ahead of you so make plans to live it to the fullest. Don't get me wrong; your period can be a pain, inconvenient and a party pooper at times but the changes that it brings are worthwhile. It will take a while to adjust, but once you've gotten used to how your body works and follow some simple rules you'll be fine.

If you haven't started your period, be happy and enjoy; don't wish these pre-puberty days away. Your change will come and when it does there will be no turning back.

THE SEEDS OF CHANGE

A NUMBER OF SIGNIFICANT AND subtle changes will take place in your body as you start your transition from childhood to womanhood. These changes will affect the way you think, look and feel. This isn't something you can stop from happening; they will take place whether you are willing to participate or not. Rather than worry about this, embrace this period in your life (smile). A caterpillar can look cute, but it doesn't stay that way. Its destiny is to become a beautiful butterfly that emerges out of its protective shell (its chrysalis) just as you are emerging and blossoming into a pretty, talented, confident young woman.

Your body is in its chrysalis form. Just as the wings of the butterfly can be seen in the latter stages of the chrysalis, so too your body is showing signs of developing into a beautiful woman. You're not there as yet; you still have much to learn; however, with careful research, planning, preparation and following sound advice, you'll see that these stages are necessary for your development to becoming a woman.

The prospect of entering puberty may cause some girls to be understandably unsure of themselves; there are a number of reasons why they may feel a little apprehensive. Some girls think they won't be their parents' little girl anymore, and they were quite happy with their childhood. They may sense that a lot will now be expected of them; others may think it is too early for them to start growing up, while some feel that things are never going to be the same again. The reality is things are going to change, more will be expected of you, but these are the necessary steps that all girls have to take. It can be hard to accept, but life never stays the same.

You are a woman in training; you will learn that there is a time for everything. You need to change in order to move on and experience brand new things. That said, even though you are now an adolescent you are going to have fun. Every stage in your life adds a new facet to who you are. I had a fantastic time in my teenage years despite having to deal with seeing my period; I mean no one enjoys having to wear pads for five to seven days out of every month. It just means you will have to make adjustments. Don't let this trouble you; talk to your parents/guardians or a person you feel you can confide in about your concerns. While it is good to have a chat with your friends about the matter, talk to a person that has gone through this transitional period of change before. They will be able to encourage and help you as you go through this transformation.

This book aims to give you an insight into the changes that starting your period will bring. It is an aid to help you to manage and embrace the challenges that you will undoubtedly encounter when you start your period, which is also called menses. So let us examine what these transformations are.

THE ORGANS THAT CAUSE PUBERTY TO BEGIN

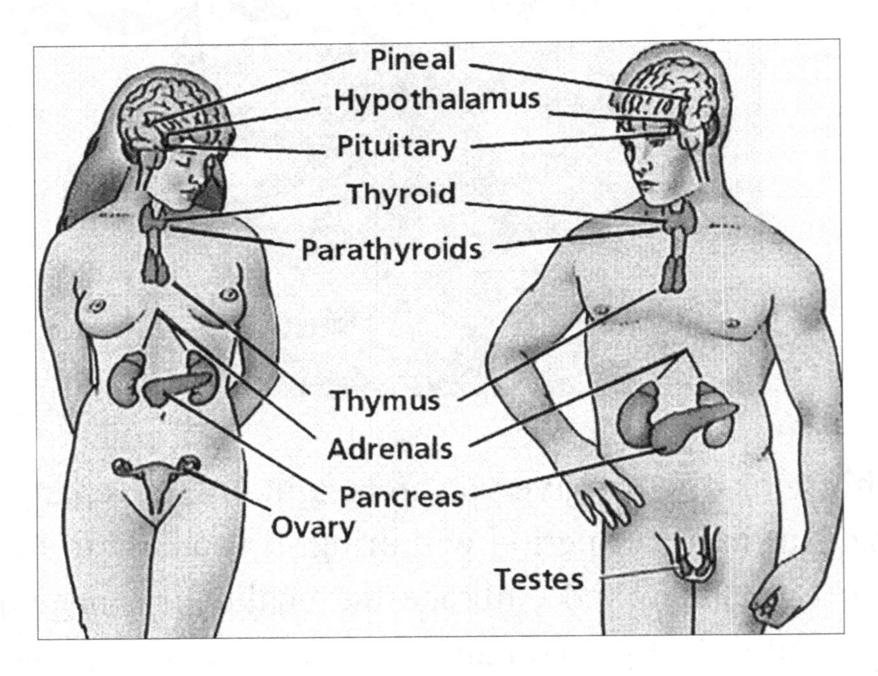

Fig.1. The organs of the endocrine system

The diagram above (fig.1) identifies the principal organs of the endocrine system. The glands of the endocrine system and the hormones they produce influence almost every cell, organ and functioning of your body. The system is essential for regulating your mood, growth, development of organ function and your body's metabolism.

An endocrine gland is an organ that secretes special messenger chemicals called hormones. The main endocrine glands responsible for causing you to start puberty are the pituitary gland, the hypothalamus gland and the gonads (sex glands) which are the testes for boys and the ovaries for girls (fig.1) The pituitary gland is also known as the "master gland," so called because it makes hormones that control several other endocrine glands, including the ovaries. It is these glands that are directly accountable for the changes that take place within you.

Hormones released from the endocrine glands act as your body's chemical messengers, transferring information from one set of cells to another. Although there are many, hormones will only work on the cells that they were made to act and respond to.

IT'S ALL ABOUT TO CHANGE

YOUR BODY WILL GO THROUGH two types of changes as a result of puberty: developmental and cyclic changes; it's a change within a change.

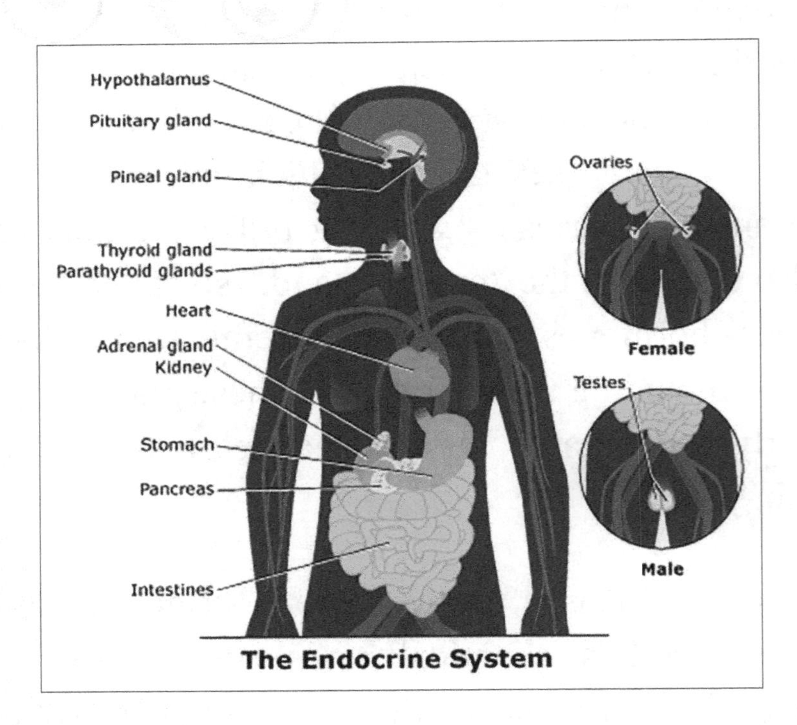

The Endocrine System

Both changes are influenced by hormones of the endocrine system. The hypothalamus, pituitary glands, and the ovaries are largely responsible for the growth and development that take place as a result of puberty. These include: making your bones strong, breast development (from having no boobs to buds and finally having breasts), changes in body shape, muscle formation and toning, changes in your skin, and the presence of pubic hair among other things.

Cyclic changes take place as a result of your monthly period (menses). They are influenced by the hormones produced by your now mature ovaries. These two types of changes will occur at the same time in the early stages with the cyclical changes continuing until your period ends (known as menopause).

The hormones that your body produces during puberty influence each other. An example to help you understand how these hormones work together and depend on each other would be to look at the function of a car battery. All cars need a battery to enable it drive and function. In order for a car battery to remain charged it needs the car to be driven regularly. This in turn charges the battery, so it can keep the car driving. For cyclic changes to take place, the pituitary and hypothalamus glands must be functioning properly, so that the hormonal signals will be sent to the ovary to produce two very important hormones called estrogen and progesterone.

DEVELOPMENTAL CHANGES

THERE IS SOMETHING SPECIAL ABOUT a woman's breasts; it is one of the most striking differences between you and boys, and the most prominent feature of a woman. When puberty begins your breasts may become more developed and increase in size. The time for this change differs from person to person. Some will begin to blossom prior to the arrival of their period while others don't start until their late teens. This may have been on your wish list for ages and as soon as your breast buds appear you're whisking your mother to the nearest department store to purchase that first bra. Your breasts may become sensitive to touch almost to the point of pain; the area around the nipple will also increase in size with the area surrounding your nipples (the areole) becoming darker.

Your body shape will become more defined; you will begin to lose the "puppy fat" you once had, and you'll notice your legs will lengthen.

It's an exciting time as you recognise the change in yourself. Hallelujahs are being echoed throughout the world because the attributes that girls have been praying for have arrived.

In addition to the curvier you, the appearance of pubic hair is also evident, with the hair becoming coarse. This change is not always welcomed by girls, especially as it will not be uniform; but don't worry, it will even out.

The underarm hairs will also be making their appearance; many girls, including my daughter, find this most distasteful.

Your body is amazing. The hormones produced during puberty will cause you to have dramatic growth spurts; some teens will wake up and find that they'd grown almost an inch overnight! Sometimes the changes will be gradual but charted over a short period of time they can be equally dramatic. A typical example of this is seen in your shoe size. Consider this scenario to illustrate my point. Your mother brought you a pair of shoes two months ago that you couldn't wear because they were too big; your feet were practically swimming in them. (Typical mothers always buying things for their children to grow into!)

You came across them while you were tidying your room and decided to try them on to see how long it would be before you could wear them, only to find they are the exact fit! You'll see this repeated in the clothes you wear. This is the perfect excuse to get a new wardrobe of clothes. Yippee!

MUM, WE NEED TO GO SHOPPING!

Your skin will also undergo changes. Fluctuating hormone levels due to your menstrual cycle can cause you to develop acne, which ranges in severity from the odd zit appearing to worrying about possible scaring. Thankfully, in cases of mild acne, there are a number of over the counter and natural solutions to treat this problem.

These developmental changes will continue into your late teens and sometimes into your early twenties. During this time, some girls often complain about feeling awkward in their bodies; they notice the changes and at times feel out of sorts because they don't know

what is happening. Fortunately you can now recognise that this is as a result of your hormones, and you are not alone. Eating fresh fruits and vegetables, drinking water and taking regular exercise can help regulate and keep the effects of these hormonal changes at bay.

CYCLIC CHANGES, THE SWITCH HAS BEEN TURNED ON

CYCLIC CHANGES TAKE PLACE AS a result of hormones that are secreted from the hypothalamus and pituitary glands. Their job is to act on your ovaries, forcing them to mature and in turn produce their own unique hormonal messengers. This triggers the start of your period. It's as if a number of switches have been turned on in your body. The hormones produced by your now functioning ovaries are estrogen and progesterone. They work in harmony with two other hormones produced by the pituitary glands, LH and FHS. Their role is to prepare your body on a monthly basis for the releasing of a mature egg for fertilisation (ovulation), and possible pregnancy. (Fig.2)

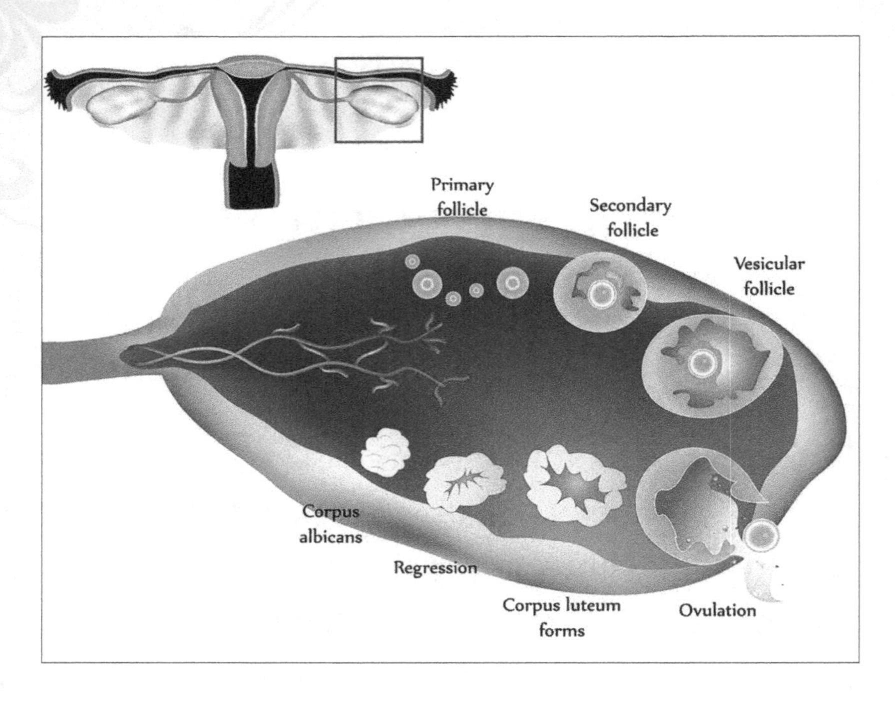

Fig.2 Female Ovary showing ovulation step by step

These same hormones also send signals to the womb to shed the lining that would have been necessary if your egg had been fertilized by a sperm, as a result of sexual intercourse taking place (fig.3). The shedding of this lining is what constitutes your period (menses) and lasts for an average of between 5-7 days. The length of your monthly cycle ranges from 25-35 days with the average being 28 days. The diagram below (fig.3) illustrates the menstrual cycle in detail, corresponding to the activity of the ovaries. It charts the changes that take place in your womb leading to the menstrual flow. This diagram also shows the differing levels of the four principle hormones that are involved during a typical 28-day cycle. (Don't worry if this diagram seems complicated now; as you get older you will find it quite informative.)

When you initially begin your period, the cycle may not be regular. For the first few months your cycle may be as short as two weeks, or as long as 40 days. The length of your menstrual flow may also differ; this is to be expected as your body is adjusting. As a result of these hormones being produced, your body goes through a series of physical and chemical changes that affect your body and mind. These transformational changes can cause the following symptoms to occur: irritability, loss of concentration, headaches, depression, mood swings, bloating, pain

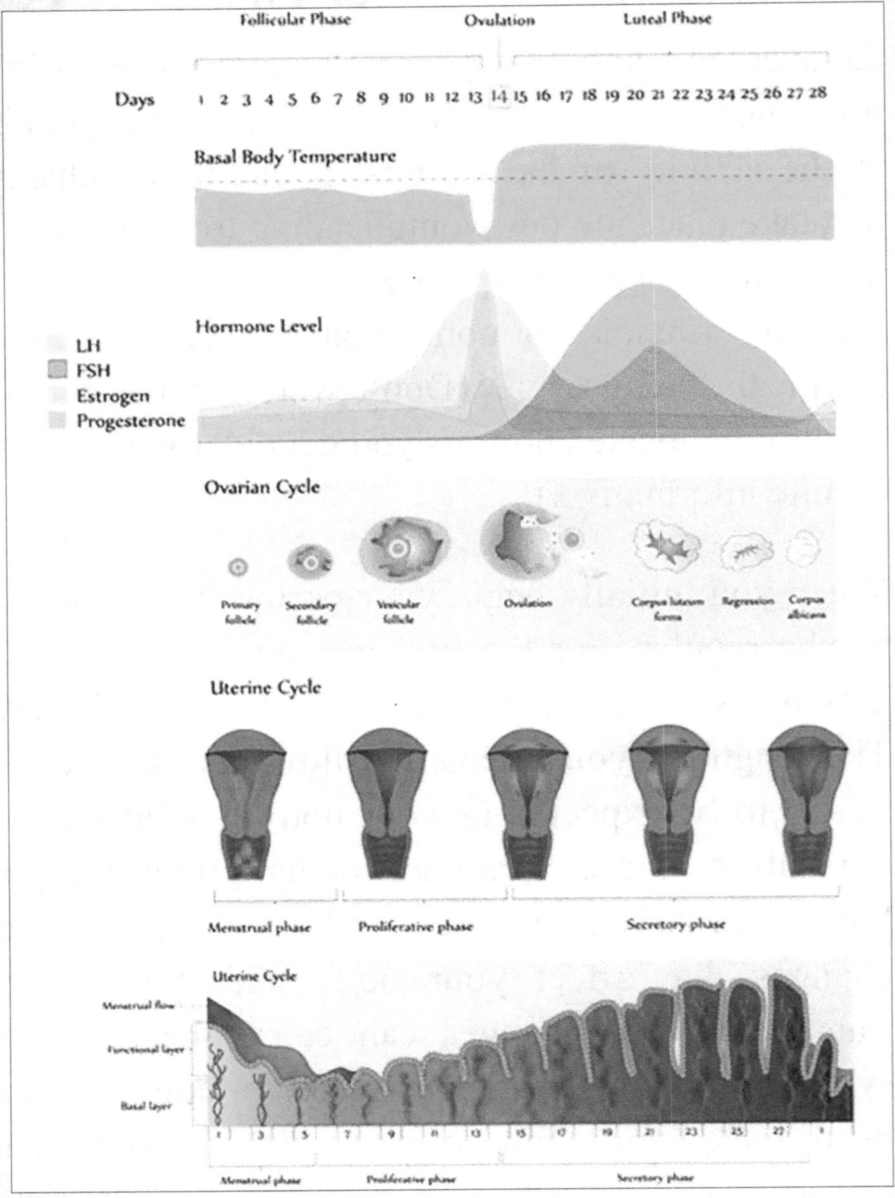

Fig.3 Diagram showing Uterine and Ovarian Cycle, Hormone level and Basal body temperature Ovulation

in the legs, nausea, lower back ache, breast tenderness and or enlargement (yes, more enlargement), crying for no apparent reason, stomach cramps, vaginal cramping and tiredness. It can also cause you to have food cravings, usually for something salty or sweet. These symptoms form parts of what is known as PMS (premenstrual syndrome).

You may be one of the lucky ones and have no symptoms at all, while others may only have a few, which vary in severity, but most will experience some of the above mentioned symptoms due to these cyclic

changes at some point over the coming years. Mild forms of PMS are quite common; however, if they are severe or last beyond your period, speak to your parents and seek medical advice.

CRY ME A RIVER

LET ME SHARE ONE OF my experiences with you. A few days prior to the start of my period, I was making my way to my room and saw a tiny piece of paper on the floor. I wept. "How could the paper be on the floor creating a mess?" I sobbed "Why didn't somebody pick it up? It is so unfair." Gut-wrenching wailing could be heard coming from my house, which went on for a few hours.

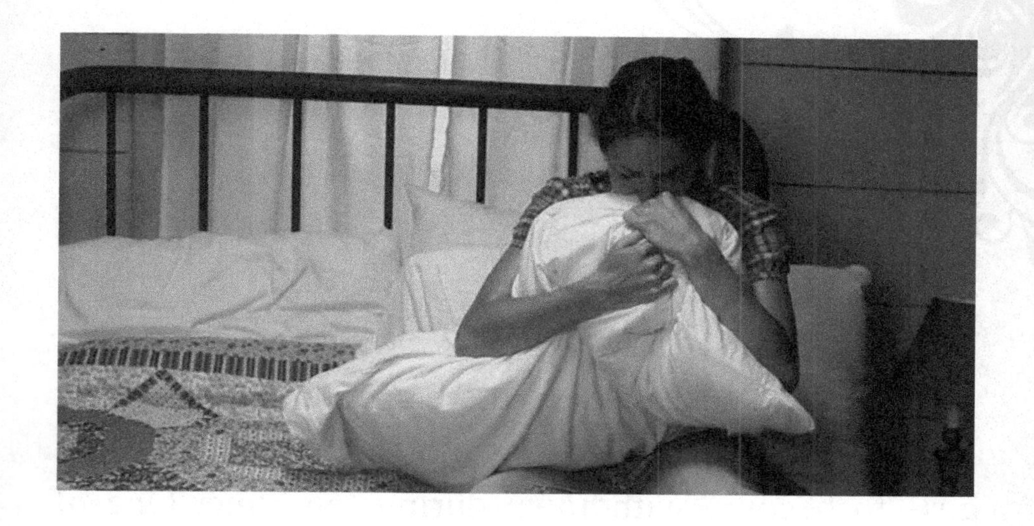

I was so glad no one was at home at the time. I knew it didn't make any sense but I was powerless to stem the tide of sorrow that engulfed me as I sat looking at this tiny piece of paper.

I was behaving as if somebody close to me had gone away or, worse, died; I couldn't understand why I felt that way until my period arrived a few days later. Your body can catch you off guard at times.

THE TEENAGE RETREAT

WHILE OTHERS ARE ENJOYING THE transformation of their bodies, there are some that are not so happy. It is quite common for some girls to become withdrawn during this time. One of the reasons that this happens may be because the transformations are taking place for all to see, and they wish it to be more private. It can cause some girls to feel uncomfortable. I mean one day you're as flat as a pancake the next you're sprouting these breasts that just keep growing, so it does take a bit of getting used to. This reminds me of the story, "The magic porridge pot" when the boy forgot the words to tell the pot to stop cooking and the porridge started flowing down the town's street. There are times when you want to put a pause on your physical development.

You want to have some time by yourself so you can take in the changes. I remember feeling decidedly self-conscious and shy when my breasts started to grow. Both my younger siblings went through a similar experience when they entered puberty.

BEAUTY AND THE BEAST

I HAVE SPOKEN TO MANY parents who have raised concerns about their teenage daughters. "She was such a lovely child, but I don't know what has happened to her since she became a teenager. She hardly talks to me and just goes straight to her room; she's moody and is sometimes rude." This beauty versus the beast syndrome where you become irritated and moody is quite common in women and is not restricted to adolescents. However, mood swings as a result of puberty do not give you license to be rude. Difficult as it may be, self-control needs to be implemented at all times. Think before you speak, as words spoken cannot be taken back. If you are experiencing any problems, it is really important to find someone that you can confide in, so you can both work out a plan to help solve them.

RESPONSIBILITY AND PERSONAL HYGIENE

The beginning of your period means you have to become more responsible. This is something you didn't have to concern yourself with before. Dependent upon the age that you start your period, it will now be your duty to ensure you have enough sanitary wares as you do not want to run out of them. To promote this practice, ask your mother for an allowance if you don't already have one, to buy your personal hygiene products. This will give you a sense of pride and boosts your self-confidence. Monitoring your period is extremely helpful. To assist you with this task, you will need a diary. Begin by jotting down the date you started your period and when you finished. When you continue monitoring

in this manner, you will notice a pattern emerging. This allows you to determine how long your cycle is likely to be, and whether it is a typical 28-day cycle or not, and you will be able to observe how long your period lasts. These two pieces of information will in turn enable you to predict when your next period will be. This ability will be of tremendous value as it removes the guess work; it puts you in control and allows you to plan ahead. Taking notes of any feelings or emotions that you experience during your cycle can be a remarkably useful tool to help you understand your body and the changes you go through prior to, during and after your period. But more importantly it will help you recognise these symptoms and put in the actions plans so that you avoid getting caught off guard. I have included a period planner and a diary at the end of this book.

There are a wide range of sanitary products available for you to buy and try out, as not all pads are created equal. A lot of girls do react to some pads as they cause irritation. This is because the materials they use to make the pads prevent air from reaching your skin. The lack of oxygen in addition to the materials in the pad reacting with your skin causes a condition known as dermatitis.

I would advise you to use pads that are made from natural materials such as cotton or other natural fibres as they allow your skin to breathe. These types of pads tend not to be produced by the major companies that you usually see in your supermarkets. So search around in your local health store.

Many companies will send you free samples of their pads to try out. Make use of these offers, as you'll need to find a product that is right for you, and you may as well save some money.

There are a lot of sanitary pads available for you to choose from. I would not advise you to use tampons when you first start your period. There are a number of reasons:

1. Your vaginal wall is very sensitive and tight. Your body needs to adjust to becoming a woman.
2. Using tampons can be very tricky and painful to get used to. The first time I tried using a tampon I was walking like a penguin. It hurt so much. This may not happen to you, but please allow yourself time to get used to your developing body. 
3. Tampon use has been linked to TSS (Toxic Shock Syndrome) a disease caused by a bug that produces a toxin that can make you very sick. If it gets into your blood it can cause serious problems and even cause death.

Dependent on your age, I would wait a year to 18 months before using tampons. In addition there are now other alternatives to pads and tampons. Please check out my website

www.GirlsItstimeForAChange.com

You will notice that your vagina produces secretions, and sometimes there is an odour. Your vagina is a self-cleaning organ with its own lubrication to ensure it stays clean and healthy, removing bacteria and products that are harmful. Do not use soap and absolutely DO NOT DOUCHE. Douching involves squirting liquid into your vagina. Using soaps in your vagina and douching causes an imbalance, which upsets the natural pH of this organ. This can cause infections that can be very dangerous and painful. To ensure that you maintain a healthy vagina just clean the outside of the vulva area. This is made up of the pubic area where you have pubic hair growing and the entrance to the vagina, which is protected by two folds of skin known as the labia minora and majora.

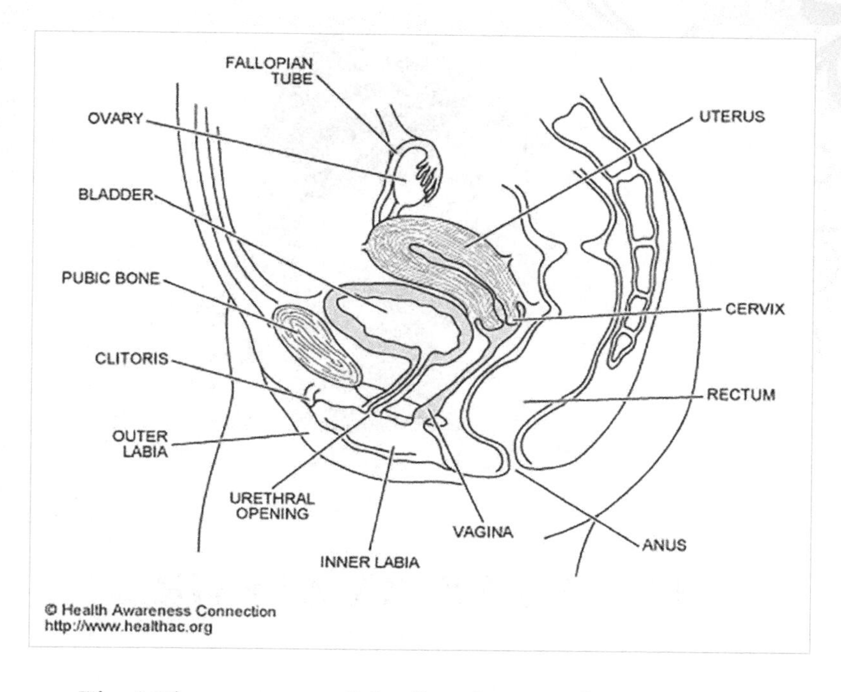

Fig,4 The anatomy of the female reproductive organs

www.GirlsItstimeForAChange.com

IT'S A SWEATY AFFAIR

UNDERSTANDING HOW YOUR BODY ODOUR changes during your menstrual cycle is a must. Personal hygiene needs be taken seriously as your self-esteem can suffer if you don't follow some basic guidelines. People judge one another by how a person looks and how they smell.

The truth is, being on your period stinks; I mean that literally as well as figuratively. Sweating changes drastically with the onset of puberty, and you will sweat more. Sweat glands are found all over your body, there are two types; the eccrine and apocrine sweat glands. Both types of glands are controlled by the sympathetic nervous system, which controls many of your involuntary actions such as breathing, heartbeat and sweating.

The apocrine glands are switched on at puberty. They are found in your armpits, genital area, the palms of your hands and the soles of your feet. These apocrine glands' secretions will cause to you to smell, well, how can I put this nicely, smelly? You see the bacteria that are normally found on your skin break down the sweat produced by the apocrine glands, and this is what causes body odour. Washing daily, especially when you are on your period, changing your clothes and using deodorant are essential. No matter how nice a personality you may have or how pretty you look, nobody will be sticking around a person who reeks of body odour unless they've lost their sense of smell.

Endeavour to smell lovelier when you're on your period than at any other time in the month. Get yourself a pretty toiletry bag that you carry at all times, containing your favourite perfume. Ensure that you have included deodorant, some wipes, an extra pair of underwear and sanitary towels.

Whenever you can pop into the bathroom, use your wipes to refresh your underarms, and use unscented wipes to cleanse your pubic area and bum (anus) and change your pads often. A common question that is often asked by girls is, how often should I change my sanitary pads? This is dependent on your menstrual flow; change your pad at least every three hours, if you are heavy then more often. Some girls are so heavy they have to change their pads within the hour. The problem with most pads is that they do not allow air to flow so your body's normal bacteria combined with your menstrual flow can result in an unpleasant odour.

Remember these equations:

1. Sweat + Bacteria = Smelly
2. Blood + Sweat + Bacteria = REALLY SMELLY.

For more information about what pads are right for you and other information go to: www.girlsitstimeforachange.com

WHAT TO WEAR AND WHAT NOT TO WEAR; THAT IS THE QUESTION

NOW THAT YOU'VE STARTED YOUR period there are a few things that you need to be aware of when it comes to choosing what to wear on the days just before and during your period. As I've already stated, your period is dependent on various chemical messengers (hormones). As a result, just before their period is due some girls may feel bloated, their breasts may get bigger and they may feel uncomfortable. If you are experiencing this, not to worry;

things will get back to normal once your period begins. The bloating that you may sometimes experience can cause your clothes to feel tight. This, coupled with the period blues that affects some girls, can be hard. To avoid this here are a few tips that will help.

Tip. 1 Because of the bloating that is sometimes experienced try to avoid tight fitted clothing. Look in your closet and sort out some of your outfits that are loose fitting; failing that ask your mum for her help in buying some fabulous clothes that are loose fitting so during that time of bloating you and you can wear them and feel comfortable. (A legitimate excuse for more shopping.) I don't mean you have to go and buy a tent. Buy tops, skirts or dresses that are cut on the bias. (The garment is cut at an angle instead of on the grain of the fabric) Here is an example of what I mean. The garments are made by cutting diagonally against the fabric's grain direction.

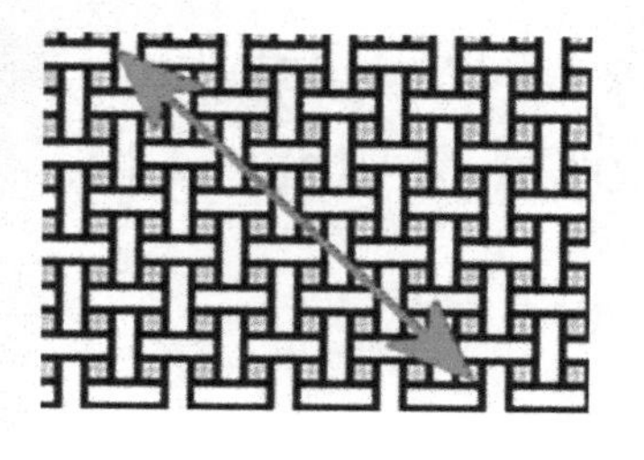

When you buy garments cut on the bias, it gives a natural flow and stretch when you wear them, which means when you're feeling bloated your clothes won't pull and they will fit nicely. This comes in handy when you are wearing a buttoned top as it helps to avoid gaping across your chest. You can wear your favourite dress even if you are bloated, as it will stretch without looking as if it is. All this helps to keep you feeling great and helps keep the period blues from visiting and taking up residence.

Tip. 2 If you are like some girls whose breasts becomes bigger a week or so before their period begins, it may be advisable to buy a bra that is one cup bigger, that

you can wear during that time before you're due to come on. This makes it more comfortable for you, and your nipples, which can become very sensitive, will be less painful. In addition you won't have the spilling over effect that is sometimes seen when a person wears a bra that is too small.

Tip. 3 Avoid wearing white or bright coloured skirts, jeans, trousers or dresses just before you start your period and definitely not when you're on. Funny thing with me: I always had this urge to wear white at that time. It's as if my body was trying to catch me out. Using your period planner will help you to know when this will be. I would suggest three to four days before you're due as your period can come on early. 
If you unavoidably have to wear white before or during your period, ensure you wear a panty liner or pad just in case you have

started, taking the time to pop into the bathroom to check that everything is okay. White is a lovely colour, especially in the summer, but a spot of red really does show itself.

Does that mean you have to be looking drab during your period? No, of course not! But you will have to make adjustments. Wear a dark coloured skirt, trouser or jeans; the dark colour will help to absorb the stain and so help avoid embarrassment. Wear a dark coloured bottom but brighten it up with a bright coloured top. No one will be the wiser and you'll feel confident knowing you've got things under control.

Tip. 4 Don't wear your pretty underwear when you're on your period as they can become soiled. It is very hard to get bloodstains out. Use dark coloured underwear or disposable ones so if they do become soiled it won't be a problem.

Tip. 5 Always walk with your emergency pack containing two or three pads, a spare pair of underwear, travel pack of wipes and deodorant with you. You never know when you or somebody you know may start their period early or forget to bring pads with them.

Suppose I start my period early and don't have a pad; what can I do?

Tip. 6 If you find that you have started your period, go into a toilet, fold some toilet paper over about fourteen times so that it looks like the shape of a pad, and use it until you can get to a store where sanitary pads are sold.

What happens if I have started my period and it has come through to my clothes?

Tip 7. Accidents do happen. If this occurs and you're in a public place, put on your coat or jacket or use your friends. Or tell a woman what has happened and ask for their help. If your jacket is short put the jacket around your waist, and if you don't live far get home. Preferably use a disabled toilet, and wash out your soiled items. Many toilets have automatic driers so you can use them to dry your clothes. Where there are no disabled toilets then use the woman's toilet. It can be embarrassing but remember you're not alone, and this has happened to countless women all over the world.

If all else fails call your mum, sister, friend or family member to pick you up.

All these tips are to help you navigate your way around the obstacles that sometimes pop up as you start becoming a woman. Use them and you will be happy that you did.

BE CAREFUL OF THINGS THAT INFLUENCE YOU

THE MEDIA WILL BOMBARD YOU with images of super-thin models and a large choice of products convincing you that they have what you need to be successful. At all times throughout your life you will be exposed to magazines, books, music, movies and adverts that subtly imply you're not good enough and that you need to buy, wear, or have this product to improve yourself. A week or so before your period begins, as previously mentioned, you may become irritable, moody, and maybe a little depressed. Reading such articles during this time, in particular, will do little to help lift your mood or boost your confidence.

I should also point out that your hormonal levels are influenced by your mood. I'd advise you to stay away from these media forms, which try to portray models or celebrities who look a certain way or act in a particular manner as your gold standard to reach in life. You have no idea what they've had to do to reach there, and you don't even know if they are happy. Do not believe everything you read. A lot of models and celebrities have been airbrushed to make them look perfect. It is a technique used by photographers and editors to remove so-called "flaws." They can use this method to remove spots and other blemishes, and it is even used to make a model or celebrity look slimmer, taller, have longer legs or slimmer arms. So looks can be deceiving. The goal of the media today is to present you with a product or idea that you are to buy into. Their aim is to make you to spend, regardless of personal cost to yourself. Self-worth must be guarded at all times. If media, celebrities, etc, are constantly telling you that a particular body shape is to be attained or having a certain product will enhance your image, whether your body is predisposed to be that way or not, then you may want to have that shape or have that product at all cost. There are countless young girls who have lost their lives in pursuit of the "perfect" shape due to anorexia nervosa.

THINS FAST!
The Perfect Body
How to LOSE WEIGHT

This is a devastating disease that causes an individual to see themselves as fat, which then leads the individual to either go on extreme diets or stop eating altogether. This disease has a profound effect upon the life of the sufferer and her family. There are many girls who are battling with anorexia nervosa, bulimia nervosa and other eating disorders.

Here, are some startling statistics from The US department of Mental Health. The same is true for other countries like The United Kingdom.

- *The mortality rate associated with anorexia nervosais 12 times higher than the death rate of ALL causes of death for females 15–24 years old.*

- *Anorexia is the 3rd most common chronic illness among adolescents.*

- *95% of those that have eating disorders are between the ages of 12 and 25.*

- *50% of girls between the ages of 11 and 13 see themselves as overweight.*

The majority of people are affected by what they see on TV, videos, advertisements and other forms of media.

It is so important that you're around people who will inspire you and encourage you. Don't waste your time chasing after things that bring no real joy to your life and will not help to make you a better person. Speak positivity into your life every day; say to yourself "I am special, I have a lot to achieve, and I aim to be the best." Do not measure yourself against other people because you will either come up short, which will affect your self-confidence, or you can become self-centered. When you're feeling down, go out, pamper yourself, watch a comedy with your family or friends, have a laugh and don't take yourself too seriously. Humour works wonders for you by lightening your mood, especially when the period blues comes knocking.

A SELF-AWAKENING

YOUR MENSTRUAL CYCLE GIVES RISE to an awareness of yourself and your environment; you will begin to see things differently over the coming years. Your opinions, thought patterns and value systems that were primarily fashioned from those of your parents will gradually be replaced by your own experiences and thoughts. Your ability to deal with your monthly period and the challenges it presents will determine how you'll tackle difficulties and challenges you will undoubtedly face in life. Learning to overcome these obstacles by finding solutions will bring enormous rewards to you, and it is a skill that is extremely useful for you to learn.

SCALES FALLING FROM YOUR EYES AND A WORD OF CAUTION

YOUR VIEW OF THE OPPOSITE sex can be quite perplexing, and change literally overnight, from seeing them as a nuisance that you barely tolerate, to becoming intrigued, interested and attracted to the same past pain in the butt.

The change from "Oh boy what a bother" to "Oh boy isn't he fine!" is perfectly normal; there is no need to think you've been taken over by an alien or something equally as extreme. Your body is developing into a woman, and the obvious reason for your transformation is preparing you for becoming pregnant and childbirth. In order for you to be successful, you've being given the tools to accomplish this. You didn't think having breasts, hips and long legs were just for you to be happy did you? Oh no, they are for you to attract a mate!

The boys are also going through complimentary changes. The once choir boy voice has now been replaced with a deeper one that you find fascinating. You notice your lanky school friend is filling out, having broader shoulders, a muscular frame, hairs on his chest (if you like that sort of thing), a more angular face accompanied by facial hair; can you believe it? Your bodies have been designed to complement each other.

Okay stop right there! Apply the brakes; there are a number of reasons why you shouldn't

think about having a baby for quite some time. There is one clear deciding factor, and that is you are not a woman yet. The transformations that you are seeing in yourself and your friends are exciting and confusing. You have to make the right choices, because the consequences can be far reaching and can last a lifetime. You've just started living, and you have goals to accomplish. You have the whole world in front of you. You need to explore and do many things before ever thinking about having a child that you are responsible for. Knowing who you are and what you want out of life is really what you need to focus on. There is a popular slogan that says, “If it feels right do it!” But if you adhere to the sentiments of this slogan and follow your emotions, which are sometimes influenced by your hormones, and are not due to proper reasoning, you may do so to at great personal cost to yourself.

Have you watched the discovery channel or national geographic? Have you observed the behaviour of animals? You will notice that they prepare their dwellings before they have their offspring, be it birds, mammals, and even insects. They make it ready, be it a nest, cave, tree or den.

You are in your chrysalis stage of life, no longer the child but not quite the woman either. You have much to learn about what it takes to be a woman and life experiences will teach you just that, so when the time is right you can be a fantastic mother.

IT'S GOOD TO TALK

YOU CAN LEARN A LOT by talking about the changes that you are going through as a result of puberty and your period. Don't feel ashamed to speak to your mother, other female relatives, as well as other young women about any anxieties you may have.

Your father is also an excellent person who could advise you. Do you think he hasn't noticed you've changed? He may feel that you have left him out and has his own thoughts concerning you. Your parents and family are there to help you prepare for life's journey into adulthood. I know from experience that you may feel awkward talking about these changes to your parents; you feel that it is private, and you are more at ease when talking about this with your friends because they're going through the same changes as you.

While this has its merit, talking to someone who has been there and bought the T-Shirt so to speak will be of great benefit to you because they will be able to give you golden nuggets of information that will make your transition into adult life easier. When you then speak with your friends it will be more about problem solving and taking action rather than complaining and having no real solutions.

IIN CONCLUSION FULFILL YOUR POTENTIAL

Reading books and researching about the world around you is great as it widens your horizons and opens up a wealth of possibilities. You will no longer be restricted to your immediate space, but you will be able to look beyond what is around you. Determine to be the best in whatever you do in life. Do not limit yourself; try to imagine your life beyond the adjustments that you have to make and remember that time does not stand still. Be aware of your feelings but don't let them rule you. Enjoy your life; it is a precious gift. There are so many choices to make, so many twists and turns, highs and lows that you will experience. Take wise counsel from older women because they have walked this road before you. Fulfill your purpose in life because every one of us has one, and enjoy the change your period brings to you. Be consistent and persistent in achieving your goals because being a successful person requires these skills.

Observe the basic rules in this book and you will be able to appreciate the reasons for the necessary changes in a girl's life.

Would you really want life without having your period? I'll leave you to ponder what your answer will be.

I hope this book has helped you understand your body's transformation, why you feel the way that you do and the changes that will take place when you start your period. I am confident you will emerge from the chrysalis of adolescence into the woman you are destined to be.

For more information about your period, go to www. Girlsitstimeforachange.com.

YOUR PERIOD PLANNING CALENDAR

How to use your period planner

On the day you start your period place a tick on your calendar, noting the month. Tick each day that you are on until the day you finish. You can then put a line through the ticks from start to finish. You may not be regular at first but during the next six months to a year you will begin to notice two very important things.

1. *You will notice the length of your cycle whether it is a 28-day, shorter or longer. This will help you predict when your next period will be.*

2. *You will know how long your period lasts i.e. whether it lasts for four days, six or more.*

These two bits of information will help you to plan and prepare for your periods. This will also reduce accidents, which can occur when you may have forgotten when your next period will be. Having said that, be mindful that your period can come early. So please make sure that you carry your emergency pack with you.

	1	2	3	4	5	6	7
8	9	10	11	12	13	14	15
16	17	18	19	20	21	22	22
24	25	26	27	28	29	30	31

	1	2	3	4	5	6	7
8	9	10	11	12	13	14	15
16	17	18	19	20	21	22	22
24	25	26	27	28	29		

	1	2	3	4	5	6	7
8	9	10	11	12	13	14	15
16	17	18	19	20	21	22	22
24	25	26	27	28	29	30	31

	1	2	3	4	5	6	7
8	9	10	11	12	13	14	15
16	17	18	19	20	21	22	22
24	25	26	27	28	29	30	31

	1	2	3	4	5	6	7
8	9	10	11	12	13	14	15
16	17	18	19	20	21	22	22
24	25	26	27	28	29	30	31

	1	2	3	4	5	6	7
8	9	10	11	12	13	14	15
16	17	18	19	20	21	22	22
24	25	26	27	28	29	30	31

	1	2	3	4	5	6	7
8	9	10	11	12	13	14	15
16	17	18	19	20	21	22	22
24	25	26	27	28	29	30	31

	1	2	3	4	5	6	7
8	9	10	11	12	13	14	15
16	17	18	19	20	21	22	22
24	25	26	27	28	29	30	31

	1	2	3	4	5	6	7
8	9	10	11	12	13	14	15
16	17	18	19	20	21	22	22
24	25	26	27	28	29	30	31

	1	2	3	4	5	6	7
8	9	10	11	12	13	14	15
16	17	18	19	20	21	22	22
24	25	26	27	28	29	30	31

	1	2	3	4	5	6	7
8	9	10	11	12	13	14	15
16	17	18	19	20	21	22	22
24	25	26	27	28	29	30	31

	1	2	3	4	5	6	7
8	9	10	11	12	13	14	15
16	17	18	19	20	21	22	22
24	25	26	27	28	29	30	31

DIARY

PLEASE USE THIS DIARY TO jot down your feelings, making a note of the date. You can also use icons i.e. ☺, ☹ to note how you feel in the calendar as well as in your diary. This will help identify if you are happy, weepy or irritable at certain times of the month. Again this helps in the preparation for your period.

GLOSSARY

Acne: is a condition caused by the overproduction of sebum, the oily substance produced by the sebaceous gland, combined with dead skin and blocked pores, which is generally triggered when puberty begins. Acne varies in severity from the odd pimple (zit) to the formation of cysts that can cause scaring of the face.

Anorexia Nervosa: is an eating disorder, which is marked by an extreme fear of becoming overweight. This leads to excessive dieting, which can cause serious ill health and even death.

Apocrine glands: are sweat glands that are inactive until they are stimulated by hormonal changes in puberty. The odour from sweat is due to bacterial activity on the secretions of this gland.

Bulimia Nervosa: an eating disorder in which bouts of overeating are followed by undereating, use of laxatives, or self-induced vomiting. It is associated with depression and anxiety about putting on weight.

Chrysalis: a butterfly at the stage of changing from larva to adult, during which it is inactive and encased in a hard cocoon.

Eccrine glands: are the major sweat glands of the human body; they are found in virtually all skin. They produce a clear, odourless substance, consisting primarily of water and salt. They are active in thermoregulation (cooling of the body), which is controlled by the hypothalamus.

Endocrine Glands: are glands of the endocrine system that secrete their products, hormones, directly into the blood rather than through a duct. The main endocrine glands include the pituitary gland, pancreas, ovaries, testes, thyroid gland, the adrenal glands and the hypothalamus.

Estrogen: a steroid hormone, produced mainly in the ovaries, which plays an important role in the development of female secondary sexual characteristics such as the breasts, hips and waist. It plays a crucial role in bone density, which keeps your bones strong. It is involved in the thickening of the uterus wall lining and that of the vagina, and is instrumental in other aspects of regulating the menstrual cycle. It keeps the integrity of blood vessels and your skin and promotes heart and lung function.

Follicle-stimulating hormone (FHS): is a hormone found in humans. It is secreted by the anterior pituitary gland. FSH regulates the growth, and stimulates the process of puberty and the reproductive processes of the body. FSH and Luteinizing hormone (LH) act together in reproduction.

Hormone: a chemical secreted by an endocrine gland. It regulates the function of a specific tissue or organ.

Hypothalamus gland: located on the central area on the underside of the brain, controlling involuntary functions such as body temperature and the release of hormones. One of the most critical functions of the hypothalamus is to link the nervous system to the endocrine system via the pituitary gland. The hypothalamus is responsible for various metabolic processes and other activities of the autonomic nervous system. It synthesizes and secretes certain neurohormones, often called hypothalamic-releasing hormones, and these in turn stimulate or inhibit the secretion of pituitary hormones.

The hypothalamus controls body temperature, mood, hunger, thirst, fatigue, sleep, circadian cycles (your body clock), and the release of other hormones in the body.

Luteinizing hormone (LH): is a hormone produced by the anterior pituitary gland. In females, an acute rise of LH, an LH surge, triggers ovulation and development of the corpus luteum. It acts together with FSH and regulates the other. Just like mixing a diluted drink, you don't want it too watery or too sweet; you want it just right. This is known as synergy.

Menstruation: is the monthly process of discharging blood and other matter from the womb, which occurs between puberty and menopause in women that are not pregnant.

Ovary: either of the two female reproductive organs that produce eggs in vertebrates. The ovary also produces the sex hormones estrogen and progesterone.

Period/ Menses: is the monthly discharge from the womb, which lasts for between 5-7 days.

Pituitary gland: a small oval gland at the base of the brain in vertebrates, producing hormones that control other glands and influence growth of the bone structure, sexual maturing, and general metabolism.

Premenstrual Syndrome: is a collection of physical and emotional symptoms related to a woman's menstrual cycle. Most women of childbearing age (up to 85%) report having experienced physical symptoms related to normal ovulatory function, such as bloating or breast tenderness.

Progesterone: a sex hormone produced in women, first by the corpus luteum of the ovary to prepare the womb for the fertilized ovum, and later by the placenta to maintain pregnancy.

Puberty: the stage in human physiological development when somebody becomes capable of sexual reproduction. It is marked by genital maturation, development of secondary sex characteristics, and, in girls, the first occurrence of menstruation.

Serotonin: a chemical derived from the amino acid tryptophan and widely distributed in tissues. It acts as a neurotransmitter, constricts blood vessels at injury sites, and may affect emotional states.

Testis: either of the paired male reproductive glands, roundish in shape that produce sperm and male sex hormones and hang in a small sac called the scrotum.

BIBLIOGRAPHY

Beato, M, Chavez S and Truss M (1996). "Transcriptional regulation by steroid hormones". Steroids 61 (4): 240–251.

Crisp TM, Clegg ED, Cooper RL, Wood WP, Anderson DG, Baetcke KP, Hoffmann JL, Morrow MS, Rodier DJ, Schaeffer JE, Touart LW, Zeeman MG, Patel YM (1998). "Environmental endocrine disruption: An effects assessment and analysis". Environ. Health Perspect. 106 (Suppl 1)

Dasen, J. S.; Rosenfeld, M.G. (1999). "Signaling mechanisms in pituitary morphogenesis and cell fate determination". *CurrOpinCellBiol. 11(6): 669–677*

Francis S. Greenspan and David G. Gardner (2003). Basic and Clinical Endocrinology (Lange) Hammes

SR (2003). "The further redefining of steroid-mediated signaling". *ProcNatlAcadSciUSA100(5):21680–217*

Marco Filicori,M. Filicori (1994).Ovulation Induction: Basic science and Clinical Advances (International Congress Series)

Mauro Theodora M, Goldsmith Lowell A, "Chapter 81. Biology of Eccrine, Apocrine, and Apoeccrine Sweat Glands" (Chapter). Wolff K, Goldsmith LA, Katz SI, Gilchrest B, Paller AS, Leffell DJ: Fitzpat- rick's

U.S. Department of Health and Human Services, Ofice of Public Health and Science, Ofice on Women's Health. "Frequently Asked Questions: Acne". 2009.

U.S. Department of Mental Health " Statistics of Anorexia Nervosa in young adults." 2010

CPSIA information can be obtained
at www.ICGtesting.com
Printed in the USA
BVHW011119310520
580351BV00002B/22